Simon Reid

To Simon
from Auntie D

G000019015

A MOTOR RACING
Camera 1894-1916

Frontispiece   Loraine Barrow at the wheel of his 45hp de Dietrich during the last of the great town-to-town races—the Paris–Madrid held in May 1903. Goggles protected the motorists' eyes from the dust, but the soft caps gave little or no protection in a crash. During the race Barrow swerved to avoid a dog and hit a tree at 80mph. His mechanic, Pierre Rodez, was killed instantly and Barrow died two weeks later.

ISBN 0 7153 7160 6

Library of Congress Catalog Card Number 76–9658

© 1976, G. N. Georgano for The National Motor Museum Trust

Set in 9 on 10 point Univers Medium
and printed in Great Britain
by Morrison & Gibb Ltd, London and Edinburgh
for David & Charles (Publishers) Limited
Brunel House   Newton Abbot   Devon

Published in the United States of America
by David & Charles Inc
North Pomfret   Vermont 05053   USA

Published in Canada
by Douglas David & Charles Limited
1875 Welch Street   North Vancouver   BC

A MOTOR RACING Camera 1894-1916

G. N. Georgano

For The National Motor Museum Trust

David & Charles

Newton Abbot · London · North Pomfret (Vt) · Vancouver

Introduction

As competition lies in the soul of every man, one could almost say that motor racing began as soon as there were two horseless carriages built in near enough proximity to be able to compete against one another. Long before the petrol car era, a race was organised in Wisconsin for the local builders of steam carriages. Seven cars were entered but only two actually started, on 16 July 1878. The winner covered the 201 miles at a speed of slightly more than 6mph. In Europe there was a competition organised by the French magazine *Velocipède* in 1887, but as only one competitor turned up it could hardly be called a race.

Very different was the 1894 Paris–Rouen Trial, with its 102 entrants and 21 starters. It seems that no photographs have survived of the cars in action, but fortunately most of the competitors were photographed before the start in Paris, and a selection of these from the Delarue-Nouvellière Collection opens the gallery of photographs in this book. From 1895 onwards motor racing began to spread, and at least one major race was organised by the Automobile Club de France each year. For obvious reasons action photographs are thin on the ground in the early years, and those that do exist are stronger on the drama of speed than on pinsharp detail. The latter is very evident, though, in the static shots, for the large glass plate negatives of Edwardian days gave as fine a print as anything that has been used since.

By 1906 when the Grand Prix series began, shutter speeds of 1/1000 sec were possible so that sharper action photographs could be taken; often, however, the photographer chose a slower speed in order to heighten the dramatic effect. The flying stones inevitable when cornering at speed on the loose surfaces of the day add to this. A phenomenon of early focal plane shutters was the 'leaning forward effect' caused by the fact that if the shutter was opening from bottom to top the upper part of the car had moved a little distance after the lower was exposed by the shutter. This again heightened rather than reduced the drama in early motor racing photographs.

The high proportion of French and Italian subjects in this book reflects the greater amount of motor racing that took place in those countries during our period. Also the bulk of the magnificent Branger collection, now owned by the National Motor Museum at Beaulieu, was devoted to French and Italian races.

1

Eager for new publicity methods for his newspaper, *Le Petit Journal*, Pierre Giffard organised the world's first motor competition to attract a number of competitors, the Paris–Rouen Trial of July 1894. No fewer than 102 entries were received, many of them with highly improbable motive powers such as 'gravity', 'a system of pendulums', 'weight of passengers' and 'combination of animate and mechanical motor'. However, only 21 appeared at the start, and these had no stranger motive power than petrol or steam engines. The event was not a race, and the first prize was to be awarded to the competitor who best fulfilled the conditions of being 'without danger, easily handled and not too expensive to run'. The first car to finish, Count de Dion's articulated steam carriage, was therefore not given first prize because it required two people to handle it—the driver to steer and a mechanic to look after the engine. The prize went jointly to Panhard et Levassor and Peugeot for their petrol cars, while de Dion received second prize. Of the 21 cars which set out, 17 reached Rouen successfully—an encouraging proportion considering the primitive state of the art at the time. The photos show (1) Hippolyte Panhard's Panhard et Levassor, (2) Lemaitre's Peugeot which was the second car to reach Rouen, and (3) Roger de Montais' steam-driven three-wheeler.

2

3

In 1895 a much more ambitious competition from Paris to Bordeaux and back was organised, a distance of 732 miles. This time it was a proper race although once again the first man home, Emile Levassor, did not receive first prize as his car was only a two-seater, whereas the regulations stipulated four seats. In all, 22 cars started and 9 returned to Paris forty-eight hours or more later. Here two competitors are leaving Versailles on the outward journey; 12 is a Roger-Benz and 5 is Emile Levassor's 4hp 2-cylinder Panhard et Levassor.

Steam was still represented in racing in 1895, though without much success. Here a de Dion-Bouton steam brake driven by the Comte de Chasseloup-Laubat leaves Paris en route for Bordeaux. The count, who set land speed records with an electric car a few years later, fell out of the race at Vouvray with a broken drive shaft.

4

The Chevalier René de Knyff with the 6hp Panhard et Levassor with which he won the 1898 Paris–Bordeaux Race. This car still has tiller steering but the Panhards that ran in the main event of 1898, the Paris–Amsterdam–Paris Race, had wheel steering. An unusual feature of this car is the vestigial mudguard mounted on the leading edge of the step. Within a few years racing cars were to abandon any form of mudguard in the search for weight reduction and stream-lining.

One of the most unusual of the early racing cars was the Amedée Bollée. Built specifically with competitions in mind, it had a streamlined body and, further to reduce wind resistance, a V-shaped radiator, the first of its kind. Four of these cars were built for the Paris–Amsterdam–Paris Race of 1898 and, at the end of the outward leg to Amsterdam, Bollée cars occupied the first three places but a series of accidents on the return journey reduced their final placing to third and fifth. Note the headlamps on this car, and also the wheel steering and pneumatic tyres, both well-established features on competition cars by 1898.

8

The major event of 1899 was
the Tour de France, a 1,350-
mile race held in seven stages.
It was the longest motor
competition held so far and
included some mountainous
country in the Auvergne.
Major parts such as wheels and
springs were punched with the
Automobile Club de France's
mark before the start to prevent
their being changed en route.
Here a wheel of Count Berthier
de Savigny's Panhard receives
the treatment. This particular
car never even started, for
while travelling 'at a high speed'
along the Boulevard Haussmann
in Paris the driver swerved to
avoid a pedestrian and the car
was smashed to pieces against
a lamp-post.

The leading lady driver in early races was Camille du Gast, wife of a Paris department store owner, who raced under her maiden name. Here she is seen before the start of the 744-mile Paris—Berlin Race of 1901, in which she drove a 20hp 4-cylinder Panhard. She was accompanied by the Prince du Sagan who acted as mechanic, and finished in thirty-third place. Later she drove in the 1903 Paris—Madrid Race, and then turned to motorboat racing. She was active in charities, especially those for the prevention of cruelty to animals.

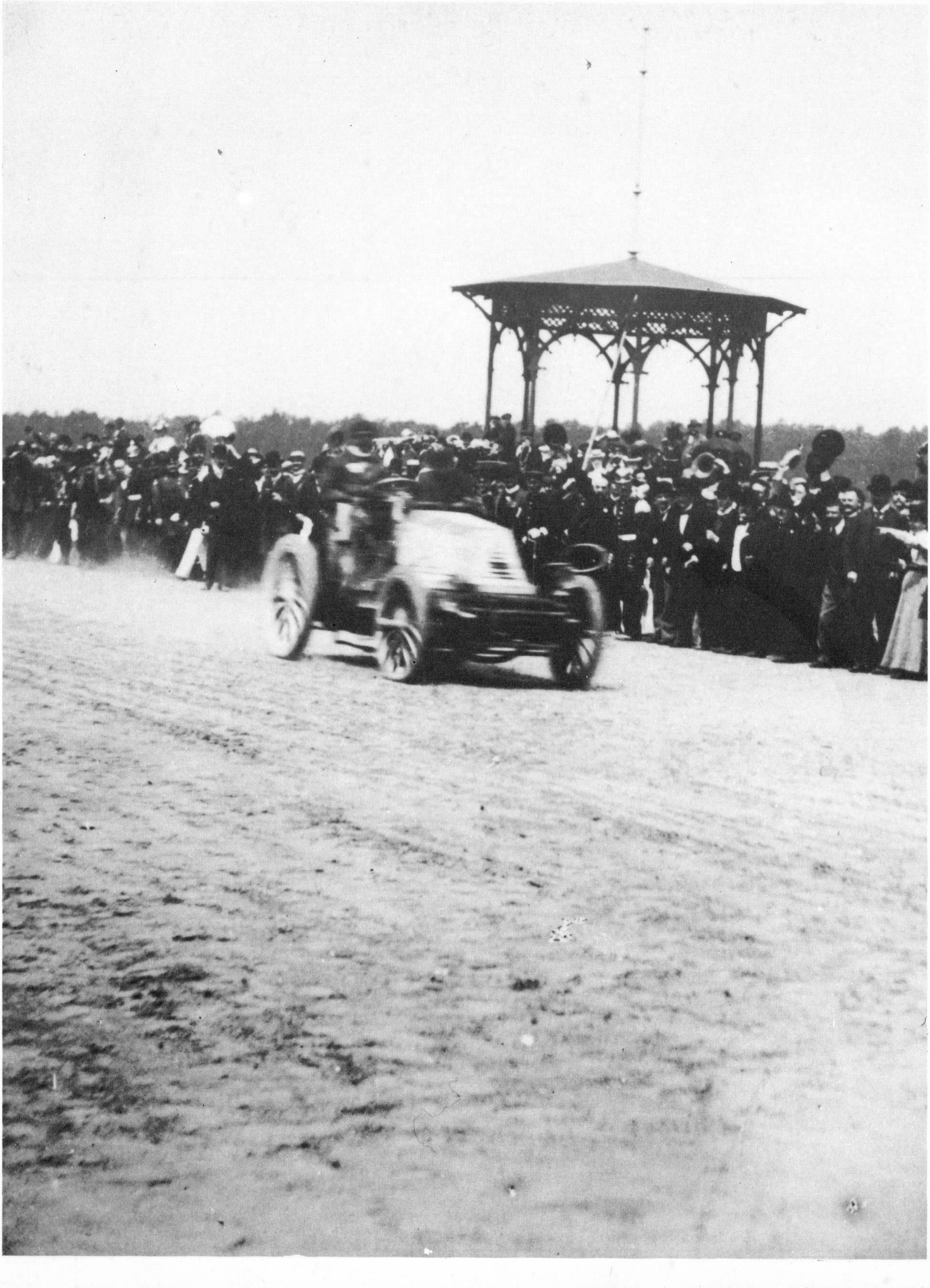

The winner of the Paris–Berlin was Henri Fournier, here seen arriving at Berlin; he averaged 44.1mph for the journey in his 60hp Mors. He also won the year's second most important event, the Paris–Bordeaux. The Paris firm of Mors was at the peak of its success in 1901, and thereafter suffered a slow decline until they abandoned racing after an unsuccessful appearance in the 1908 Grand Prix.

The largest-engined racing car of 1901 was this 17-litre 4-cylinder Napier which weighed 2 tons and was said to develop 103bhp. Fuel consumption was no more than 4mpg, so its 50-gallon tank was very useful. S. F. Edge hoped to enter it in the Gordon Bennett Race, but the regulations of this event stipulated that every part of the car should be made in the country of origin, and as the Napier wore French tyres—no British ones being strong enough to stand up to its weight —it was ineligible. Edge, here seen at the wheel, drove in the Paris–Bordeaux Race which was run concurrently with the Gordon Bennett, but fell out with clutch trouble before completing the course.

Another streamlined car in the
Bexhill Trials was the Serpollet
steam car nicknamed 'Easter
Egg', driven here by its builder,
Léon Serpollet. The car was
reputed to be doing 52mph
when the photo was taken; the
characteristic oval shape of the
wheels associated with all early
speed photographs can be seen,
although not to such an extent
as to spoil the picture.

Apart from Léon Serpollet, the best-known driver of his cars was Hubert Le Blon, seen here with his wife before starting his run at a Gaillon hill climb in September 1902. They made best time of the day with a climb at a speed of 55mph. On both sides of the Atlantic steam cars excelled at hill climbs, though seldom doing well in long-distance races.

Little attention was paid to streamlining in the early days, despite the work of Amedée Bollée, but this 1902 Mercedes driven by Baron Henri de Rothschild has a crude form of windcheating body. It was used for short-distance sprints rather than racing and is seen here during the 1902 Bexhill Speed Trials, in which it achieved fifth place in its class.

14

Each year the town-to-town races became more ambitious; the 1902 Paris–Vienna Race covered over 760 miles and crossed two national frontiers, the Franco-Swiss and the Swiss-Austrian. The actual racing distance was only 615 miles as the Swiss authorities would not allow any racing on their roads; Switzerland was more hostile to the motor car than any other European country at this time. A total of 118 cars set out from Paris, and the race was won by one of the smaller competitors, the 16hp Renault driven by Marcel Renault. *Plate 15* shows Pinson's 70hp Panhard at speed; the soldier guarding the right-hand side of the road had not prevented spectators on the opposite side crowding close to the speeding car. *Plates 16 and 17* show two of the lesser

known makes that took part in the race—Valentin's Ader (134) and Perrin's Delahaye (163). Ader was a short-lived make noted for V-formation engines. The 1902 cars were V-twins of 1,566cc capacity, but Clement Ader later went on to V-4s and V-8s (see *plate 22*). The name of Delahaye became famous in competitions from the 1930s onwards, but in 1902 they were rarely seen racing. The three 16hp cars entered in Paris–Vienna had 2-cylinder horizontal engines mounted at the front, with the cylinder heads pointing forwards, and chain drive.

16

In the endless quest for lightness
some designers of racing cars
dispensed with a body
altogether. Known as 'The
Pirate', this 1903 Oldsmobile
used the frame and engine of
the famous Curved-dash
Runabout, but seated the driver
at the back and gave him a
very long, raked steering column
in place of the tiller of the
standard model. The driver here
is William Letts, Britain's
Oldsmobile agent at the time.

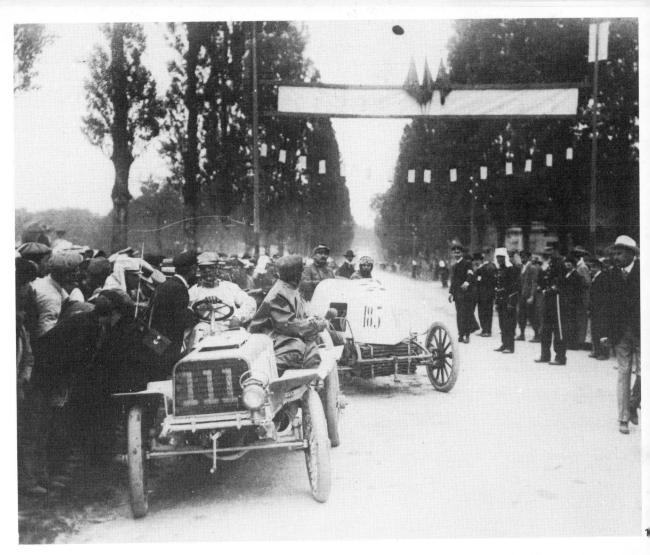

'La grandiose et meurtrière course Paris–Madrid' is how a French historian described the last town-to-town race held in May 1903. In conception it deserves the first adjective, for it was to cover 872 miles, some over roads which had barely seen a motor car at all, and to include the crossing of the Guadarrama mountains near Madrid. In effect it turned out to be 'meurtrière' as well, for an estimated ten people were killed, spectators as well as competitors, and the race was stopped at Bordeaux, less than half the distance. So adamant were the authorities that the cars were not even allowed to be driven under their own power to the railway station, but had to be towed by horses.

Here Pellison is seen in an 18hp de Dion-Bouton light car, and behind him is one of the 70hp Mors with streamlined bodies. This is Augieres' car; his team mate Gabriel was leading the race when it was stopped at Bordeaux.

Mercedes was already an important name in racing by 1903, and nine examples of the make ran in Paris–Madrid. Most of these were new 90hp models with engine capacities of 11,974cc such as this one driven by Kohler, but the best place achieved by a Mercedes was Warden's sixth with a 60hp model. Next to Kohler's car is Rigolly's 110hp Gobron-Brillié which was later the first car to exceed a speed of 100mph.

22 Camille du Gast examining the control officer's letterbox on her 30hp de Dietrich, before the start of the Paris–Madrid Race. The sealed box was for cards stamped with the time of arrival at each control point. Despite *The Autocar's* forebodings that 'we must confess to a feeling of doubt as to whether fierce long-distance motor racing is quite the thing for ladies', Mme du Gast was lying in sixth place overall when she stopped to give first aid to her team mate Stead, thus putting herself out of the running.

Clement Ader was a manufacturer of telephones who had also built an unsuccessful aeroplane, *l'Eole*. From 1900 to 1907 he made cars, most of which had V-formation engines. Beginning with a V-twin in 1900, he progressed to a V-4 in 1903, followed by a V-8 which employed two of the V-4 units coupled together in line. Despite having twice as many cylinders as any other cars in the Paris–Madrid Race, the V-8 Aders had a capacity of only 3,618cc and as they weighed less than 650kg they ran in the light car category. This is Valentin's car which finished twelfth in its class.

21

22

The first important race to be held in Belgium, and also the first important circuit race, was the Circuit des Ardennes, held over a 53-mile course which the competitors had to cover six times. After the Paris–Madrid disaster the closed circuit seemed to be the only hope for the future of motor racing, although the Ardennes race was in fact first held in 1902. Another advantage was that the spectators could see each car six times instead of only once. *Plate 23* shows a 40hp CGV passing through the small town of Bastogne, driven by Voigt, one of the partners in the firm that made it. In *plate 24* Civelli de Bosch changes a tyre on his 30hp Clement. As with the touring cars of the day, a puncture meant a change of tyre on a fixed wheel; detachable rims did not come in until 1906.

23

Two competitors at the Laffrey Hill Climb, held in August 1903. They are Wagner and Villemain who finished first and second in their class respectively, both driving stripped 20hp Darracqs. Laffrey, in hilly country near Grenoble, was one of the leading French hill climbs at this time.

The unusual windcheating body fitted to a Darracq light racing car, seen at the Dourdan Speed Trials in October 1903. The gap in the prow was supposed to reduce side pressure when negotiating corners. Even in these early days racing cars did not necessarily travel under their own power to and from the events; *plate 27* shows the Darracq after the Dourdan meeting, though horsepower was probably used only as far as the nearest railway station.

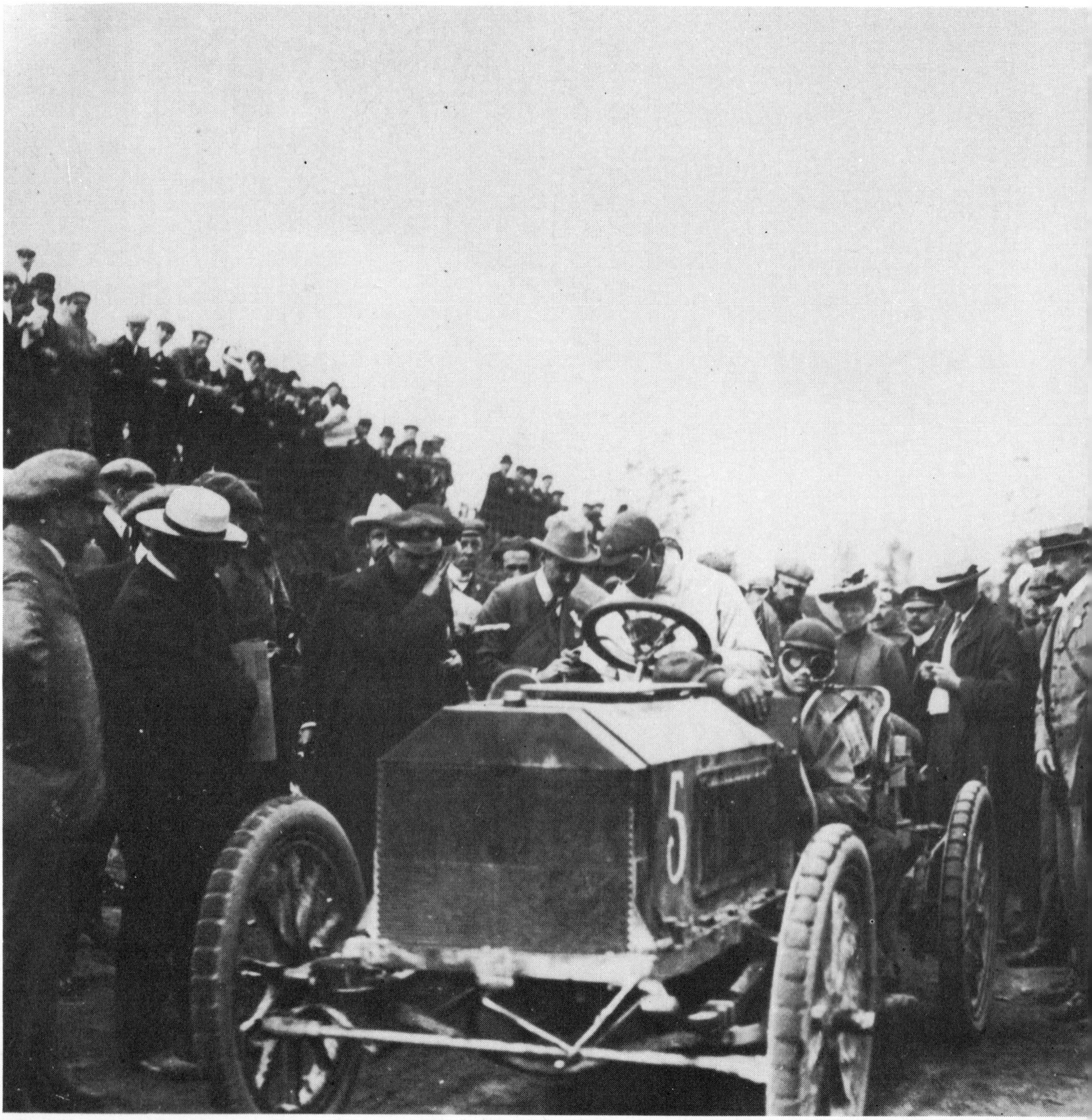

Two competitors in the 1903 Gordon Bennett Race held in Ireland. *Plate 28* shows a Napier driven by Charles Jarrott; it was this make's victory in the 1902 Gordon Bennett which gave Britain the privilege and responsibility of organising the 1903 event, but the cars from Acton did not cover themselves with glory in Ireland. Jarrott's car ran up a bank and overturned, throwing both driver and mechanic out. In his efforts to extricate his mechanic from under the car, Jarrott fainted and was thought to be dead. The American entry in *plate 29* is the 40hp Winton driven by Percy Owen. This curious vehicle had its 8½-litre engine mounted horizontally, and a 2-speed gearbox with direct drive in top. Owen's team mate Alexander Winton had an even stranger car with two of the 4-cylinder engines mounted in line, giving a capacity of 17 litres, but only one speed. Neither car did well in the race, and some unkind critics said that their only contribution was to baulk faster competitors.

The French took the 1903
Gordon Bennett Race very
seriously, and chartered the
3,500-ton steamer *Ferdinand
de Lesseps* to carry their 3
competing cars and 20 other
vehicles, together with a staff
of 100 which made the ship a
floating workshop. Here
Gabriel's Mors, the only entry
of this make, is about to be
towed away from the quayside
at Dublin.

The 1904 Gordon Bennett Race
was held over a hilly circuit in
the Taunus mountains near
Bad Homburg, and was graced
by the presence of the Kaiser
and his enthusiastic brother
Prince Henry of Prussia. The
circuit was well fenced as can
be seen here, but nevertheless
a dog has strayed onto the road
and is having a close encounter
with Henri Rougier's Turcat
Mery.

32 Steam cars were never prominent in European racing, but Léon Serpollet persevered for a number of years with his flash-boilered cars, entering them in hill climbs and sprints where they did quite well, and also in races such as Paris–Vienna, Paris–Madrid, and the 1904 Gordon Bennett Eliminating Trials. One of the cars for the latter event is shown here; it had a 6-cylinder single-acting engine and final drive by central chain. In the event none of the Serpollets were fast enough to qualify for the French team in the race.

33 The most prominent Belgian
make in the early days of racing
was Pipe, a Brussels concern
whose racing cars had the
unusual and advanced feature
of hemispherical combustion
chambers with two inclined
overhead valves per cylinder.
Here Lucien Hautvast, Pipe's
leading driver, awaits his turn at
the *pesage* before the 1904
Circuit des Ardennes. Presumably
he changed his headgear before
the actual race.

34 This impressive-looking Gobron
Brillié was one of the most
remarkable racing cars of its
era. Built in 1903 as one of the
team cars for Paris–Madrid it
was fitted in 1904 with the
windcheating prow illustrated,
and took several records in
sprints and hill climbs
culminating in the Flying
Kilometre in July 1904, when
Louis Rigolly became the first
man to go faster than 100mph,
his actual speed exceeding
103.55mph. It was still being
raced as late as 1907. The photo
shows Rigolly before his record-
breaking run at Ostend.

Hill climbs were a popular form
of motor sport from the turn of
the century onwards, and
among the best known was
Gaillon, between Mantes and
Rouen. First held in 1899, the
Gaillon meeting attracted over
100 entrants within a few years,
ranging from touring cars to the
fastest and most powerful
racing cars of the day. Here
Achille Fournier makes a
spirited climb in his Gordon
Bennett-type Hotchkiss at the
1904 Gaillon meeting.

Another Gaillon photograph, showing de la Touloubre in a Darracq awaiting his turn at the start in 1904. In order to reduce weight the car is no more than a bare chassis carrying a flimsy seat. The drilling of the sideframe members was a popular device for combating weight, but it made for a very weak structure in the event of a crash.

The most unconventional racing
cars of the era were the front-
wheel-drive transverse-engined
monsters designed and driven
by John Walter Christie, an
American engineer. His first car,
shown here, had an in-line
4-cylinder engine and was
intended to run in the 1904
Gordon Bennett Race. In 1905
Christie built a car called the
'Double Ender' with two
transverse 4-cylinder engines,
at front and rear, each driving
one axle. His final racing cars
had transverse V-4 engines, the
1907 Grand Prix entry having a
capacity of no less than 19
litres. None achieved any
success in racing, although in
1906 Christie made the fastest
time of the day in a sprint at
Ormond-Daytona Beach.

37

As in 1904 there were so many
entrants for the three places
allocated to each nation for the
Gordon Bennett Race that
Eliminating Trials were held in
Britain and France. Twenty-four
cars from ten manufacturers
contested the French trials,
including this 90hp Renault
driven by the Hungarian
ex-enginedriver Ferenc Szisz.
Underslung frames made these
Renaults lower than any of their
contemporaries; they over-
heated in the trials and were
not selected to represent France.

England's Eliminating Trials in
1905 did not attract such a
variety of makes or designs as
those of France, there being ten
cars from five manufacturers.
The cars illustrated represent
two schools of thought from
the Wolseley factory, the
horizontal-engined car (no 4)
which was the last of a series
of such designs by Herbert
Austin, and the vertical-engined
Siddeley (no 10) which
represented the new régime
brought about by the replacement
of Austin by J. D. Siddeley who
had always favoured the vertical
engine. Despite being a more
modern design, the Siddeley
was not in fact chosen to
represent Britain in the race,
this honour going to the two
Wolseleys and a Napier.

41 The 1905 Gordon Bennett was held on a mountainous circuit in the Auvergne, of which *The Car Illustrated* said, 'To describe it in detail would be something like detailing a "loop the loop" performance'. Each lap measured 85.35 miles, and had to be covered 4 times. There were numerous tortuous hairpin bends, including one in the village of Rochefort in which it was said that the owners of the house on the inside of the corner could see a car passing the parlour window and run to see the same car passing the kitchen window. This photo shows Clifford Earp on the 80hp Napier accelerating away from one of the many corners.

The winner of the 1905 Gordon
Bennett Race was the Frenchman
Léon Théry driving a 96hp
Brasier. He had also been the
victor in 1904. Earlier in his
career he had collided with a
cow which earned him the
nickname *Mort aux Vaches*, but
the regularity of his lap speeds
in the 1904 Gordon Bennett led
to the more flattering soubriquet
Le Chronomètre. Here his car is
having a change of tyres at the
depot in the Col de la Moreno.

t d'Auvergne; Coupe Gordon Bennett 1905 · LYTTLE (Pope Tolédo) Amérique

ndelle, Paris

America was represented in the 1905 Gordon Bennett by a Locomobile and two Pope-Toledos, all conventional 4-cylinder cars with chain drive. The Pope-Toledos had 2-speed gearboxes which was hardly wise in view of the mountainous nature of the course. The car illustrated, driven by H. H. Lytle, finished in twelfth place but his team mate, Albert Dingley, retired during the first lap.

The most important early race in
Italy was the Coppa Florio for a
cup presented by Cavalier
Vincenzo Florio, who later
organised the much more
famous Targa Florio. The 1905
race was held over a course
through Brescia, Cremona,
Mantua and back to Brescia.
Here Vincenzo Lancia on a
FIAT trails a fine cloud of dust
outside Cremona.

44

Stanley and White were the two best known makes of American steam car, and of these White was the more prominent in racing and hill climbing. Beginning with a lightly modified touring car in 1901, White racers became steadily more specialised, the most famous being 'Whistling Billy' (*plate 45*) whose construction was supervised by Webb Jay, the leading White driver. The engine was identical to that of the largest White touring car, but the boiler was one of greater capacity, and the special underslung frame made it the lowest racing car of its day. The name was inspired by the curious sound given off by the burners in damp weather. Jay had many successes with this car, including setting a new world track record for the mile (48.6 seconds) achieved during a race at Morris Park, New York, in July 1905. *Plate 46* shows a cruder-looking car with conventional frame at the 1907 Fort George Hill Climb, with Walter C. White at the wheel.

In 1906 the Automobile Club de France organised a new race to replace the defunct Gordon Bennett series, and called it the Grand Prix. The most unpopular feature of the Gordon Bennetts, the restriction of three competitors from each country, was abolished, and a total of thirty-four cars were entered, mostly from France, although there were also representatives from Germany and Italy. Victory went to Ferenc Szisz driving a Renault, which had the inestimable advantage of detachable rims. The hot weather, high speeds and bad surfaces destroyed the tyres in one or two laps, and drivers were constantly changing them; while most had to struggle with stiff covers and security bolts, the Renault team simply undid eight nuts, removed the rims and replaced them with new ones carrying ready-inflated tyres. This photo shows Szisz before the start.

One of the best known venues for speed events in America was the stretch of sand between Ormond and Daytona Beach, Florida, which provided a course of hard-packed sand 15 miles long and 500 feet wide. It was first used in 1902 and within two years had become an important fixture in the social and racing world. Among the cars to compete was this unusual twin-engined Mercedes in which Herbert L. Bowden was the first American to exceed 100mph. His speed, achieved in 1905, was 109.65mph over a mile, but the American Automobile Association refused to accept it as a record as they claimed the car was overweight. Named 'Flying Dutchman II', Bowden's car was lengthened to accommodate the second Mercedes engine, which came from a speedboat.

In order to avoid the carnage of
Paris—Madrid the Grand Prix
organisers completely sealed
the roads in towns and villages
with boards of fencing along all
the pavements. Here G. Teste
on a Panhard et Levassor
passes through the village of
Connerre.

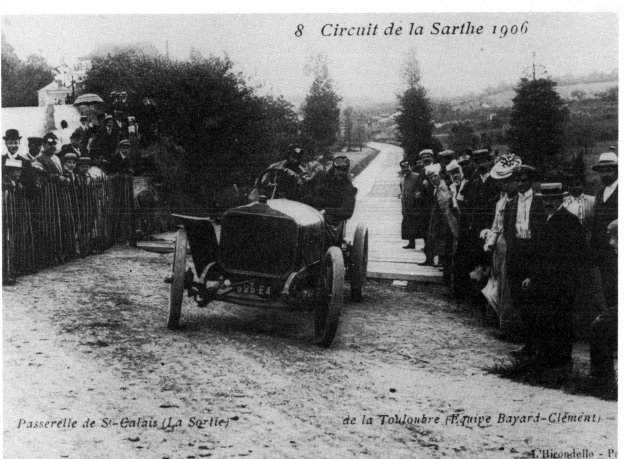

8 Circuit de la Sarthe 1906

Passerelle de St-Calais (La Sortie) *de la Touloubre (Équipe Bayard-Clément)*

L'Hirondelle - P

Another way to avoid the hazards of racing through built-up areas was to make a temporary by-pass. This was done at Ste Calais where a wooden road was laid down in the fields. This photo shows de la Touloubre's Bayard-Clément at the point where the *passerelle* rejoined the ordinary road. This must have been taken during a pre-race reconnoitre as the car carries no racing numbers, and the offside mudguard was not worn during the race itself.

9 *Circuit de la Sarthe 1906*
Passerelle de St-Calais

*Hémery et de la Touloubre
franchissant la Passerelle à 120 kilomèt.
à l'heure*

Another view of the *passerelle*
at Ste Calais, showing the
simple wooden construction,
with some spare planks piled
at the side of the road.

In the days when a maximum weight limit was the only restriction on entry to a race, the weighing-in or *pesage* was a vital part of pre-race activity. For the 1906 Circuit des Ardennes the *pesage* was held at the railway station at Bastogne. Among the cars visible here are Albert Clément's Bayard-Clément (no 3), Camille Jenatzy's Mercedes (no 4) and Otto Salzer's Mercedes (no 15). The car with the exposed engine in the foreground is a Darracq, possibly that of Louis Wagner, the race winner.

53 Brasier were not among the makes to adopt detachable rims in 1906 (the only others to do so apart from Renault were FIAT and Itala), so drivers and mechanics had to remove the old tyre, usually by cutting it with a knife and tearing off the remaining shreds with their hands. Here Pierre Bablot's pit crew are changing tyres during the Circuit des Ardennes. Note the pile of fresh tyres ready for use in the background.

America's leading race was the Vanderbilt Cup, held on various circuits on Long Island from 1904 to 1909. Crowd control was always a problem with over 250,000 spectators and only sixteen policemen per mile to control them. Here some spectators have taken to telegraph poles and rooftops to see Louis Wagner, the winner of the 1906 race, cornering in his 110hp Darracq.

Another Darracq, this time the enormous 22½-litre V-8 car built for sprints and hill climbs which took the Land Speed Record at 109.65mph in 1905 and later raised it unofficially to 117.66mph. The engine consisted of two blocks of the 1904 Gordon Bennett 4-cylinder unit mounted in V-formation and developing 200bhp. This was nearly twice the power of the contemporary Grand Prix cars, and it was put in a light chassis nearly a foot shorter than that of most Grand Prix cars. Here Algernon Lee Guinness makes adjustments to the car before climbing Gaillon hill in 1906.

The first Targa Florio organised in Sicily by Cavalier Vincenzo Florio, for production cars costing less than 20,000 francs for the chassis, took place in 1906. The definition of 'production' was that at least 10 similar chassis had to be made. The first race was poorly attended, but in 1907 a much larger field of 46 entries was received, establishing the race as one of the leading ones in the calendar—a position it has held ever since. *Plate 56* shows the Isotta Fraschini team outside their HQ in Termini, attended by goatherds and their charges. *Plate 57* is a typical Targa Florio scene, showing the mountainous country and poverty-stricken villages through which the route passed. The car is a Zust driven by Maggioni and the village is Petralia Sottana.

As a curtain-raiser to the Targa Florio, Vincenzo Florio organised a race for voiturettes three days before, and drove one of the little cars himself. This was a single-cylinder de Dion-Bouton in which he finished second. He would have won had he not entered a Sizaire-Naudin for Louis Naudin to drive, which duly took first place.

The Kaiserpreis was in some
ways Germany's answer to the
Targa Florio, being for cars of
nominally touring type with a
capacity limit of 6 litres. Held in
1907 only, it attracted far more
entries than the Targa, a total
of 92 including many from
makers whose names were not
familiar in competition lists.
Two eliminating trials were
held, the first 20 cars in each
competing in the final. *Plate 59*
shows a French-built Rochet-
Schneider driven by Viton
which made it to the final but
retired on the fourth lap. In
plate 60 two German NAGs and
a Belgian Imperia (40A) enter
the *pesage*, and in *plate 61*
Carlo Maserati's Bianchi leaves
the *pesage*. Carlo was the
eldest of the five Maserati
brothers who played such an
important part in motor racing
and gave their name to one of
Italy's best known sporting
marques.

A group of cars before the start of the 1907 Grand Prix, held on a triangular course near Dieppe. In the foreground is a 4-cylinder Darracq with v-radiator (D2) and behind it a Panhard which, in this year only, had a 'coal scuttle' type bonnet with the radiator behind the engine. Neither car did particularly well in the race, which was won by Felice Nazzaro's Fiat.

Another 1907 Grand Prix
photograph, showing Laxen's
straight-eight Weigel at the
Dunlop tyre depot. The London-
built Weigels had two 40hp
4-cylinder engines coupled
together, with a total capacity
of 14,886cc, 2-speed gearboxes
and shaft drive. Two were
entered in the race, but neither
distinguished itself. The 1907
Grand Prix saw quite a collection
of unorthodox cars, others being
the 12,750cc straight-eight
Dufaux from Switzerland and
the 19,891cc V-4 front-wheel-
drive Christie from America.

The first recorded motor race in Russia took place in 1898, the winner being Mazi in a Panhard, but the first important long-distance races were the St Petersburg–Moscow events of 1907 and 1908. The roads were appalling and more cars fell out with broken springs than with any other single defect. Of the 29 entrants in the 1908 event, only 10 reached Moscow. The winner was the Frenchman, Victor Hémery, who averaged 51.4mph in his Benz. In *plate 64* he is seen astride the finishing line. Winner of the smallest class for cars of up to 86mm cylinder bore was the Austrian Otto Hieronymus, seen in *plate 65* in his Laurin-Klement in St Petersburg before the start.

There had been classes for light cars in most of the early town-to-town races from 1900 onwards, but the peak period for voiturette racing was 1906 to 1910, when events such as the Grand Prix des Voiturettes, Coupe des Voiturettes (or Coupe de l'Auto) and Sicilian Cup attracted much bigger fields than the Grand Prix proper. In the 1908 Grand Prix des Voiturettes, held on the same circuit as the senior race but one day earlier, there were 64 entries of which 47 presented themselves at the starting line. Two of the more obscure entrants seen at the *pesage* were Menard's La Joyeuse (*plate 66*) and Thieulin's Thieulin (*plate 67*).

One of the highest-quality light
cars to take part in the Grand
Prix des Voiturettes was the
Isotta-Fraschini, powered by a
4-cylinder 1,208cc engine with
a single overhead camshaft. The
engine was said to have a
maximum speed of 3,400rpm,
a very high figure for the time.
Here is the team of 3 cars lined
up before the start, the drivers
being Buzio, Trucco and Carlo
Maserati. Buzio had the best
race, finishing in eighth place.

Mishap during the 1908 Grand Prix des Voiturettes; the Demeester driven by Martin collided with the temporary bridge set up over the road at Eu, 'both car and driver being badly damaged' according to *The Autocar*. Soon after the accident, the car was carried off the course by soldiers who were often present at races.

Two scenes from the 1908 Grand Prix: in *plate 70* the Mors driven by Camille Jenatzy leaves the paddock for the starting line, followed by George Heath's Panhard (16). This race was the last Grand Prix entered by both Panhard and Mors, two of the greatest names in the sport a few years earlier. *Plate 71* shows Paul Baras' Brasier in the pits. Note the three spare tyres carried by the car, and the stern warning against smoking in the pits.

DEFENSE EXPRESSE
DE FUMER
DANS les RAVITAILLEMENTS
sous Peine
D'EXPULSION IMMÉDIATE

British participation in the 1908
Grand Prix was limited to 3
London-built Weigels and 3
Austins, of which Moore-
Brabazon's is shown here.
Brabazon himself described the
100hp 6-cylinder Austin as 'not
really a racing car at all, but a
very fast tourer', and although
two of the cars finished, they
were well down the list,
Brabazon being best in
eighteenth place. Herbert
Austin hedged his bets in the
chains versus shaft drive
controversy, two of the cars
having propeller shafts and the
other chains.

Awaiting his turn to make an ascent of Gaillon hill in 1908 is Count Sascha Kolowrat in his Laurin-Klement, which was the most successful small Austrian competition car of the pre-1914 period. Kolowrat, owner of a Bohemian glassworks, was a colourful character who carried a pet piglet in the back seat of the Laurin-Klement which he drove in the 1913 Alpine Trial.

Itala was a make that made a considerable impact on motor racing in the pre-1914 era, with cars that were generally conventional except that they used shaft drive from the start in 1904 at a time when most powerful machines still favoured chains. This is the 12-litre 4-cylinder car driven by Allesandro Cagno in the 1908 Grand Prix and Coppa Florio, seen on the weighbridge before the latter event. This is almost certainly the car which came to England in 1909 or 1910 and was fitted with a four-seater body by Vincents of Reading. It is today owned by Cecil Clutton and Jack Williamson and makes regular appearances in Vintage Sports Car Club events.

Second place in the 1908 Coppa Florio was taken by Vincenzo Trucco who drove a French-built de Dietrich. Here he is leaving the *pesage* at Bologna before the start of the race, in which record speeds were achieved thanks to the straight roads. The fastest lap was covered at over 82mph by Vincenzo Lancia, while the winner Nazzaro averaged 74.1mph. As in several other events at this time, the *pesage* was held at the railway station where there was a convenient weighbridge.

Itala's great rival, and generally the more successful, was Fiat. Here is the car which won the 1908 Coppa Florio driven by the very successful driver Felice Nazzaro who, the previous year, had won all three of Europe's major events, Grand Prix, Targa Florio and Kaiserpreis. Note the vast funnel used in the replenishing of the fuel tank.

Because of the demise of the
Grand Prix there was no big
car racing in France in 1909 or
1910, but the Coupe des
Voiturettes—or Coupe de
l'Auto as it was sometimes
called after the magazine that
sponsored it—continued to be
held. Twenty-one cars faced
the starter on the Boulogne
circuit; the photograph of Jules
Goux' 2-cylinder Lion-Peugeot
shows the thick fog which
caused the start to be postponed
by thirty minutes, despite the
fact that the race was held on
Midsummer Day.

77

The day after the Coppa Florio
another event was held on the
same course, the Targa Bologna
for cars of Targa Florio type—
closer to production touring cars
than the Grand Prix machines.
The winner seen here at
Bologna was Porporato driving
a French-built Berliet which
had the smallest engine of any
car in the race.

Some enthusiasts called Brooklands Motor Course the Eighth Wonder of the World, and although the 2¾-mile banked concrete track in Surrey aroused considerable hostility from local residents when it was built in 1907 its value was soon realised, not only for sport but also as a testing place for new cars. In the original races the cars did not carry numbers and the drivers wore different coloured jockeys' silks for identification. This made identification of the cars difficult and within a few months of the opening, the cars began to be numbered. This line-up on the Railway Banking, c 1912, includes Singer, Sunbeam and Vauxhall cars.

From the beginning Brooklands
was used for record attempts
as well as for racing, and in fact
S. F. Edge had set a new
record at the track one week
before any racing began at all.
This photo shows a 3-litre
Sunbeam at its depot by the
Members' Bridge during a
record attempt in 1912.

The high speeds obtainable at Brooklands encouraged the development of streamlining. *Plate 81* shows a Straker-Squire with pointed tail and the cowling over the radiator which was a very popular device. At the wheel is Roy Fedden, the designer of the 15hp Straker-Squire and later to be responsible for Bristol aero engines. The submarine-like vehicle in *plate 82* is J. E. Hollebone's 25.9hp Diatto. The air vents in the side of the bonnet look as if they had been cut open with a tin opener.

81

82

This curiously high and narrow
Peugeot seen at the start of the
1911 Mont Ventoux hill climb
is a modified version of the
4-cylinder racing Lion-Peugeot
of 1910, with the very long-
stroke cylinder dimensions of
65 x 260mm. It has been fitted
with a different radiator and
sketchy four-seater body. At
the wheel is the well known
Peugeot driver Georges Boillot.

In the absence of the official Grand Prix in 1911, the Automobile Club de l'Ouest organised a race which they called the Grand Prix de France on the Le Mans circuit. Entries were so few that they could not afford to be choosy, so a completely free formula was allowed. Among the cars which did turn up were a 5-year-old Lorraine-Dietrich, a 4-year-old Corre-La Licorne and a Bugatti which was new but very small, with an engine capacity of less than 10% of the Lorraine-Dietrich's 18 litres. The race was won by a 10-litre Fiat which was a tuned standard model, driven by Victor Hémery who was apparently not deterred by carrying number 13.

Nearing the summit of Mont
Ventoux in 1912 is a 4-cylinder
Hispano-Suiza, the touring
model of which was known as
the Alfonso XIII after the
Spanish monarch who owned
several of them, and was
probably the greatest motoring
enthusiast among all Europe's
kings. These long-stroke
(80 x 180mm) Hispanos had
many successes in hill climbs
and voiturette races. On this
occasion Grua climbed the
13¼-mile hill in 22min 50sec.

In 1912 the Grand Prix proper
was revived, and concurrently
with it was run the Coupe de
l'Auto for smaller cars of up to
3 litres' capacity. Peugeot's
entries for the latter were much
more up to date than their 1911
offerings had been, with a new
4-cylinder engine which had
4 inclined overhead valves per
cylinder, operated by overhead
camshafts. They also had shaft
drive, and were in many ways
smaller versions of Peugeot's
Grand Prix cars. In the event
only 1 Peugeot ran in the Coupe
de l'Auto, and 3 in the Grand
Prix, which Georges Boillot's
car won. Réné Thomas' 3-litre
car, seen here at a pit stop,
retired.

A tyre depot on a barge was an unusual sight at any time, but this was the location for the Continental Tyre Company at the 1912 Belgian Grand Prix. Detachable wheels were commonplace by this date.

The first country after France to organise a national Grand Prix was Belgium, who held a two-day event totalling 720 miles in July 1912. It did not attract a very exciting international entry, but several local makes such as Minerva, Miesse, Germain, FAB and SAVA took part as well as 3 sleeve-valve Mercedes-Knights and a lone example of a Model T Ford. The Ford, which did not figure in the results, is seen here on the paved streets of Dinant driven by Catala who later made cars under the name of Alatac.

One of the three SAVAs which took part in the 1912 Belgian Grand Prix. They were conventional 4-cylinder side-valve-engined cars little different from the firm's touring cars and did not cover themselves with glory, none of the team starting on the second day. The Grand Prix was really more of a reliability trial, for there was no outright winner. Cars which maintained an average speed allotted to them on a cubic capacity basis were awarded points, highest marks going to the Minerva and Mercedes teams, both using sleeve valves.

Two competitors in the 1913 Le Mans cyclecar race, Anthony's Violet-Bogey and Muraour's Ronteix (nos 43 and 45 respectively). Both were relatively sophisticated in having water-cooled 4-cylinder engines, although their final drive was by single chain. In the race the Ronteix was first and a sister car to the Violet-Bogey came in second.

Compared with the Grand Prix proper, these cyclecar races were very light-hearted and informal affairs; in the Amiens race the Morgan mechanic Frank Thomas, feeling thirsty, asked the driver to stop by the crowd of spectators, one of whom offered a swig from his bottle of wine. The driver, W. G. McMinnies, joined his mechanic in a quick tipple before carrying on with the race. Despite, or perhaps because of, this unscheduled refuelling stop, they won the race.

A popular light car which took
part in many competitions was
the 6hp Peugeot, known as the
'Bébé'. Although built by
Peugeot it was designed by
Ettore Bugatti and was the last
design which the great man did
for a company other than his
own. Its most unusual feature
was the transmission which
consisted of two concentric
propeller shafts, one revolving
inside the other, which meshed
with two rows of teeth on the
crown wheel to give the two
forward speeds. Three 'Bébés'
ran in the 1913 Le Mans
Cyclecar Grand Prix, and one
of these is seen here cornering
energetically at a hill climb,
possibly Mont Ventoux.

American cars were unfamiliar sights in European racing in the years immediately before World War I, although there had been Gordon Bennett and Grand Prix entries by such firms as Christie, Locomobile, Pope-Toledo and Thomas a few years earlier. The only Americans to be seen in the Coupe de l'Auto races were two Buicks entered in 1913 and driven by the Frenchmen Repusseau and Drouillet. Buick were no strangers to racing in their own country, winning many stock car races from 1908 onwards, and also racing at Brooklands where a special event for the marque was organised in 1912. The Coupe de l'Auto was not a feather in their cap, however, and both cars retired before the finish.

Britain's oldest motor race, the Tourist Trophy, was first run in 1905 as an event for stock touring cars which had to carry four-seater coachwork. It continued in this form until 1908, after which there was a lapse of six years before it was again held. Still located in the Isle of Man, the 1914 TT was a two-day event for cars of a maximum capacity of 3,310cc and minimum weight of 2,300lb. The cars were no longer particularly touring in character and the Sunbeams, one of which won the race, were smaller versions of the firm's Grand Prix cars. This photo shows K. Lee Guinness' winning Sunbeam. Note the sketchy wing on the offside only, to protect the driver from flying stones.

The London firm of Straker-Squire entered two cars in the 1914 TT, one of which was fitted for the practice period with a new engine with four valves per cylinder and a single overhead camshaft. It proved troublesome and for the race itself both cars employed side-valve engines which had been kept in reserve just in case. R. S. Witchell's car, seen here on the weighbridge, finished a creditable fourth, behind the Sunbeam and two sleeve-valve Minervas.

96 Two less well known competitors
in the 1914 Tourist Trophy,
Lisle's Star (no 5) and the
broken-down Hudson of
Rawlinson (no 10). The Stars
were conventional machines
with short-stroke versions of
the standard 20.1hp engine, but
they did not do so well in the
race. Lisle's car hit a wall in the
sixth lap, and shortly before his
team mate Crossman had
retired with a water leak. The
Hudson, an unmodified stock
chassis, fared even worse and
was the only car which failed
to start.

The 1914 Grand Prix is famous
because of the heroic struggle
by Georges Boillot to defeat
the Mercedes team, and the
precision organisation of this
team which foreshadowed that
of Mercedes-Benz under the
great Alfred Neubauer in the
years 1934–39. Several months
before the race, technicians and
drivers had visited the course
and what they saw of the
terrain undoubtedly influenced
the final design of the cars.
Even so, they brought several
alternative rear axle ratios for
the practice sessions and, as
one observer put it, 'enough
spare parts to put together a
couple of engines'. They were
rewarded by a 1–2–3 finish,
and the eclipse of French cars
seemed a worrying omen for
the Great War which was to
break out only one month
later. The photograph shows
Salzer's Mercedes which
finished in second place.

The cars which Peugeot entered for the 1914 Grand Prix were among the most advanced in the race, having twin overhead camshaft engines with four inclined valves per cylinder in a hemispherical combustion chamber, and also four-wheel brakes. Three cars were entered, that of Georges Boillot leading until the eighteenth lap when he was overtaken by Christian Lautenschlager's Mercedes, only to retire in the twentieth and final lap. Peugeot construction did not seem to be up to the advanced design, for Boillot's car was practically falling to pieces, with worn-out and inoperative front brakes and the steering column broken away from its mounting. The photograph shows Boillot's team mate Jules Goux taking the hairpin at Sept Chemins.

99 The career of the 1914 Grand Prix
Mercedes was by no means
ended by the outbreak of the
Great War. One went to
America and, driven by Ralph
de Palma, won the Chicago
Cup and Elgin Trophy in 1914,
the Indianapolis 500 in 1915,
and races at Des Moines,
Minneapolis, Omaha and
Kansas City in 1916. He is seen
here receiving the chequered
flag at Indy in 1915. Other cars
from the Mercedes team (five
were built) ran in the 1922
Targa Florio, Count Masetti's
car winning the race, and they
were still competing successfully
in hill climbs as late as 1927.
In the 1920s some of them
were fitted with front-wheel
brakes and superchargers.

99

00

America's answer to Brooklands was the Indianapolis Motor Speedway, on which construction began early in 1909. Unlike Brooklands with its irregular shape and choice of circuits, Indy is rectangular in layout, with four identical $\frac{1}{4}$-mile turns to a lap of $2\frac{1}{2}$ miles. Racing began in August 1909 but the race with which the Speedway is always associated, the '500', was not held until 1911. It was limited to cars of not more than 600 cu ins capacity (9,832cc), and 46 entries were received. This figure was reduced to 40 by a qualifying test in which each car had to average 75mph over one of the straights, and qualifying events have been a feature of most '500' races. Since 1912 the number of entries has been fixed at 33. Another feature of the first race which has survived to the present day is the pace car, a touring car behind which the competitors cover one lap before accelerating to their full speed. In later years the pace car has been awarded to the winner as one of his many perquisites. *Plate 100* shows the start of the 1911 race, with the Stoddard-Dayton pace car on the right in the front line, and next to it is Lewis Strang's Case (no 1), Ralph de Palma's Simplex (no 2), Harry Endicott's Interstate (no 3) and Johnny Aitken's National (no 4).

Plate 101 shows the first turn in the same race, Louis Disbrow's Pope-Hartford (no 5), and the two Cases of Joe Jagersberger (no 8) and Will Jones (no 9).

A new element was introduced into American racing with the board tracks. The first of these was built in 1910 at Playa del Rey, California, but it was burned to the ground in 1912 and it was three years before any others were built. From 1915 to the late 1920s, however, the board tracks flourished, at least 23 being built all over the United States, from Sheepshead Bay, Brooklyn in the East to Tacoma, Washington, in the West. They varied in size, but a typical one was a mile and a quarter in length, with the banking as steep as 52°. This was much steeper than the 9° 12′ of the Indianapolis brick track and allowed very high speeds, though there was always the danger of cars going 'over the top'. Here two Peugeots driven by Ralph Mulford (leading) and Dario Resta are seen at the Sheepshead Bay track in 1916.

Acknowledgements

I would like to thank Mr Michael Sedgwick for reading the manuscript and making many useful comments, my wife for checking the manuscript, Mr Brian Coe of the Kodak Museum for information about early cameras, and Mrs Judy Steele for typing the manuscript and coping with last-minute additions and alterations. All the photographs are from the National Motor Museum, with the exception of the following:
Autocar: 9, 10, 12, 13, 21, 25, 26, 27
Automotive History Collection, Detroit Public Library: 48
Indianapolis Motor Speedway Association: 99, 100, 101, 102